ROCK STARS

ROCKS

By Chris and Helen Pellant

Gareth Stevens
Publishing

Please visit our web site at **www.garethstevens.com**. For a free catalog describing Gareth Stevens Publishing's list of high-quality books, call 1-800-542-2595 (USA) or 1-800-387-3178 (Canada). Gareth Stevens Publishing's fax: 1-877-542-2596

Library of Congress Cataloging-in-Publication Data

Pellant, Chris.
    Rocks / Chris and Helen Pellant. — U.S. ed.
      p. cm. — (Rock stars)
    Includes index.
    ISBN-10: 0-8368-9225-9   ISBN-13: 978-0-8368-9225-3 (lib. bdg.)
    1. Rocks—Juvenile literature. I. Pellant, Helen. II. Title.
QE432.2.P449   2009
552—dc22   2008016114

This North American edition first published in 2009 by
Gareth Stevens Publishing
A Weekly Reader® Company
1 Reader's Digest Road
Pleasantville, NY 10570-7000 USA

This U.S. edition copyright © 2009 by Gareth Stevens, Inc. Original edition copyright © 2008 by ticktock Media Ltd. First published in Great Britain in 2008 by ticktock Media Ltd., 2 Orchard Business Centre, North Farm Road, Tunbridge Wells, Kent, TN2 3XF.

For ticktock:
Project Editor: Julia Adams
Picture Researcher: Lizzie Knowles

Project Designer: Emma Randall
With thanks to Sophie Furse, James Powell, Graham Rich

For Gareth Stevens:
Senior Managing Editor: Lisa M. Herrington
Senior Editor: Barbara Bakowski

Creative Director: Lisa Donovan
Electronic Production Manager: Paul Bodley

Picture credits (t = top; b = bottom; c = center; l = left; r = right):
age fotostock/SuperStock: 14br. All Canada Photos/Alamy: 12-13b. Tom Bean/Corbis: 11br. Dea/A. Rizzi/ Getty Images: 21cr. iStock: 5bl, 22ft, 23tl, 23bl. Andrew J. Martinez/Science Photo Library: 3D, 10tl. Susumu Nishinaga/Science Photo Library: 10br. Chris and Helen Pellant: 3E, F, G, H, 7tl, 7tr, 8b, 9bl x2, 12tl, 13t x2, 14tl, 15br, 16 all, 17l x3, 18 all, 19l x3, 19tr, 20 all, 21l x3. Shutterstock: 1, 2, 3A, B, C, I, J, K, 4 all, 5t, 5bc, 5br, 6tl, 7tc, 9ftl, 9tl, 9cl, 9cr, 10cl, 10-11c, 14–15 main, 14l, 17r x4, 19br x2, 21tr, 21br, 22t, 23tr, 23cl, 23cr, 23br, 24tl. Shiela Terry/Science Photo Library: 22c. ticktock Media Archive: 6–7b, 8c, 11tr, 12b, 22b.

Printed in the United States of America

3 4 5 6 7 8 9 10 09

Contents

Rock Collector

Words that appear in **bold** are explained in the glossary.

What Are Rocks?

You may not notice it, but nearly everything you stand on is made of rock! Earth's crust, or outer layer, is entirely made up of rock. Rock is under the forests and the ocean floor.

There are many different kinds of rocks. Some rocks are hard and powdery. Others are soft and easy to mold. Rocks come in a variety of colors, shapes, and sizes.

Rocks can be as big as a mountain.

Rocks can be as small as a pebble on a beach.

It's a Fact!
Sand is a type of rock. When it is heated, it can be made into glass.

The Twelve Apostles, Australia

Earth really rocks! In fact, rocks shape all the landscapes around you. The next time you are in the countryside or at the beach, see how many different kinds of rocks you can find.

People use rocks to make things. Roads, buildings, and statues are all made of different kinds of rocks. Some plates you eat from and the chalk you draw with are made of rock, too!

How Do Rocks Form?

Rocks are always forming and changing. The changes sometimes take place over millions of years. Rocks form both on the surface of Earth and underground, where it is very hot.

There are three kinds of rock. They form in different ways. **Igneous rocks** form when **molten rock** cools deep underground or on Earth's surface. When rocks are heated under a lot of pressure, they change into **metamorphic rocks**. **Sedimentary rocks** form when many tiny bits of other rocks are squeezed together.

The Rock Cycle

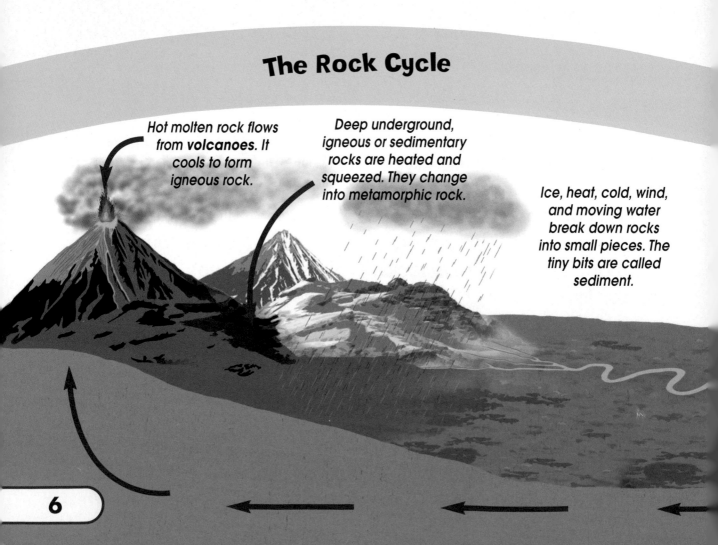

Hot molten rock flows from **volcanoes**. It cools to form igneous rock.

Deep underground, igneous or sedimentary rocks are heated and squeezed. They change into metamorphic rock.

Ice, heat, cold, wind, and moving water break down rocks into small pieces. The tiny bits are called sediment.

Three Types of Rock

igneous rock
basalt

sedimentary rock
sandstone

metamorphic rock
marble

More sediment comes from rocks along the coast. The sediment sinks to the seabed. The small pieces are pressed together and form sedimentary rock.

Rivers carry the sediment to the sea.

Sedimentary rocks are pushed down as new layers of sediment build up. Deep underground, the rock becomes hot and melts.

Igneous Rock: Granite

Granite is an igneous rock. It is formed from hot molten rock deep under Earth's surface.

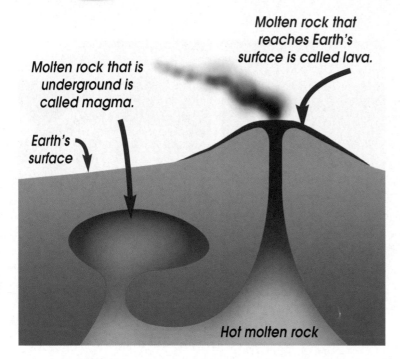

Molten rock that reaches Earth's surface is called lava.

Molten rock that is underground is called magma.

Earth's surface

Hot molten rock

Sometimes the molten rock, or **magma,** bursts to Earth's surface through a volcano. Now called **lava**, it cools and hardens.

The molten rock can also cool and harden under Earth's surface. Granite is formed from rock that cools inside Earth.

Granite Landscape

This granite is on the Isle of Mull in Scotland. Its pink color shows that the granite has a lot of feldspar in it. This granite was once beneath Earth's surface. Earth's outer layer has worn away, and now the granite is visible.

Minerals in Rocks

Like all rocks, granite is made up of **minerals**. They are the pieces of material that join to form rocks. Minerals can be many different shapes and colors. Some minerals form as **crystals**.

Granite Ingredients

Granite is made of three different minerals. Quartz is gray or white. Mica is black. Feldspar is pink or white. The three minerals were **welded** together to form granite.

QUARTZ (GRAY)

MICA (BLACK)

FELDSPAR (PINK)

Sedimentary Rock: Sandstone

Sandstone is a sedimentary rock. It is made up of many layers of sand. Sand is a type of rock, too. It is made up of minerals.

You can feel the grains when sand runs through your fingers.

You can look at individual **grains** of sand through a microscope. The grains are tiny pieces of a mineral called quartz. Sand is also made up of tiny pieces of animal shells and other minerals.

Sand grains seen through a microscope

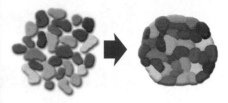

Weight of
new layers

Squeezed layers

Grains of sand   Sedimentary rock

Ice, heat, cold, wind, and moving water wear grains of sand off rocks. These grains pile up in layers. As more layers form, the layers at the bottom are squeezed together to make sandstone. This process can happen in a desert, a river, or an ocean.

Sandstone Landscape

Many layers of sand are visible in this photograph of sandstone.

Sand sometimes forms **dunes** on beaches or deserts. Sand can also form in layers on the bottom of a river or an ocean.

Metamorphic Rock: Gneiss

Gneiss (pronounced "nice") is a metamorphic rock. Metamorphic rocks form when igneous or sedimentary rocks are changed by heat or pressure or both.

Deep under Earth's surface, there is a lot of heat and pressure. The rocks there are heated and squeezed, causing them to change.

What Happens When Rocks Change?

Rocks are made of minerals. A rock changes when its minerals change. If you compare a rock before it has changed and afterward, it may look quite different!

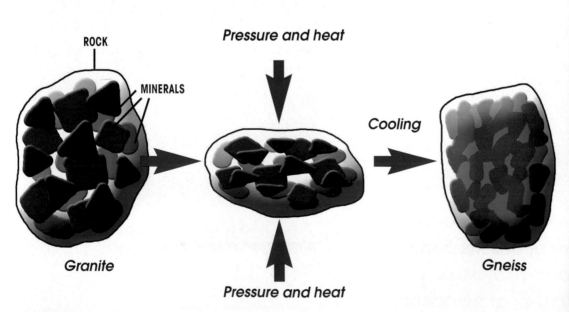

ROCK

MINERALS

Pressure and heat

Cooling

Granite

Pressure and heat

Gneiss

Gneiss
(metamorphic rock)

Granite
(igneous rock)

Compare granite with gneiss. You can see
that the mineral pattern has changed.
The minerals in granite are speckled.
In gneiss, they are arranged in stripes.

Gneiss Landscape

This photo shows an
area of northern
Canada called the
Canadian Shield. It is
mostly made of
gneiss. This region is
one of the largest
areas of metamorphic
rocks on Earth. The
rocks here are almost
4 billion years old!

Amazing Rocky Places

Rivers, rain, ice, and wind break down rocks until they crumble. This process is called **weathering**. **Erosion** happens when the bits of rock are carried away by wind, water, or ice.

It's a Fact!

Weathering and erosion make rock stacks, cliffs, canyons, and arches like the formations shown here.

Grand Canyon, Arizona

This huge canyon was carved by a river. It took more than 17 million years to form. It is made of sandstone and is more than 1 mile (1.6 kilometers) deep!

Monument Valley, Arizona/Utah

This big area of red sandstone was formed about 270 million years ago! Wind and water eroded the rock, leaving unusual formations. The rock stacks you see here are called spires. Some spires rise as high as 1,000 feet (300 meters).

Elephant's Arch, Italy

On the coast of Sicily, the sea has created this amazing natural arch. It is formed from cooled lava.

Red Lava, Iceland

These huge lava hills are bright red. Their red color comes from the mineral hematite.

Rock Collector

Andesite

MINERALS:	feldspar, mica, hornblende
FORMED:	in volcanoes, from lava
FEATURES:	fine grains of gray crystal, with larger light and dark ones

Basalt

MINERALS:	feldspar, augite
FORMED:	in volcanoes, from lava
FEATURES:	dark color, with fine grains of crystal, often full of tiny holes

Dolerite

MINERALS:	feldspar, augite
FORMED:	deep underground, from magma
FEATURES:	mostly dark, with tiny speckles of light-colored crystals

Gabbro

MINERALS:	feldspar, augite
FORMED:	deep underground, from magma
FEATURES:	many dark-colored and some light-colored crystals

Obsidian

MINERALS:	quartz, feldspar
FORMED:	in volcanoes, from lava
FEATURES:	like black glass; may have white "snowflake" patterns

Porphyry

MINERALS:	quartz, mica, feldspar
FORMED:	deep underground from magma
FEATURES:	a mix of some large crystals and many tiny ones

Diorite

MINERALS: feldspar, mica, hornblende
FORMED: deep underground, from magma
FEATURES: speckled, with large dark and light crystals

Granite

MINERALS: quartz, mica, feldspar
FORMED: deep underground, from magma
FEATURES: speckled, with large crystals in pink, white, and dark gray

Rhyolite

MINERALS: quartz, feldspar
FORMED: in volcanoes, from lava
FEATURES: hard, with sharp edges and fine, light-colored crystals

Getting Started

To collect rocks properly, you will need the right tools. One of the most important tools is a rock hammer. It is very hard. Use it to hammer only small, loose rocks.

You will also need:

- a strong backpack for your tools and the rocks you collect

- a notebook and a pen to record where and when you found the rocks

- a magnifying glass for looking at details

- air-filled packing wrap or newspaper to protect rock samples

- goggles to wear when hammering. Rock splinters may get in your eyes.

Rock Collector

Arkose

MINERALS: quartz, feldspar
FORMED: in dry areas with **flash floods**
FEATURES: pink, with large grains

Breccia

MINERALS: vary by location
FORMED: at the foot of steep hills or cliffs
FEATURES: large, sharp pieces of rock

Coal

MINERALS: none, mainly made of carbon
FORMED: in swamp forests
FEATURES: black, with shiny patches;
may rub off on hands

Conglomerate

MINERALS: vary by location
FORMED: on seabeds, in deserts or rivers
FEATURES: sand grains and pebbles of
different kinds of rocks

Fossil limestone

MINERALS: calcite
FORMED: on seabeds
FEATURES: light color; may contain **fossils**

Sandstone

MINERALS: quartz
FORMED: in shallow water, on seabeds,
or on riverbeds
FEATURES: small grains of sand; smooth,
sandy surface

Chalk

MINERALS: calcite
FORMED: on seabeds
FEATURES: white and powdery; may rub off on hands

Crinoidal limestone

MINERALS: calcite
FORMED: on seabeds
FEATURES: gray, with **crinoid** fossils

Shale

MINERALS: quartz, mica
FORMED: on seabeds
FEATURES: dark color, with some light specks; tiny grains

Finding Rocks

You can find rocks in many different places. Look near the seashore, along riverbanks, and on hillsides.

CAUTION
Always go rock collecting with an adult. Some places may be dangerous.

- Collect only loose rock samples. Do not break off large pieces.

- Use a rock hammer to break rocks into smaller pieces. Be sure to wear goggles!

- Photograph locations and large features such as cliffs, hillsides, and mountains.

Rock Collector

Eclogite

MINERALS: olivine, garnet, augite
FORMED: deep in Earth's crust
FEATURES: red and green mineral crystals

Gneiss

MINERALS: quartz, feldspar, mica
FORMED: deep under mountain ranges
FEATURES: bands of dark and light colors

Hornfels

MINERALS: quartz, mica, cordierite
FORMED: near large areas of igneous rock
FEATURES: dark color, with sharp edges

Metaquartzite

MINERALS: quartz
FORMED: near large areas of igneous rock
FEATURES: light quartz crystals; looks like a lump of sugar

Schist

MINERALS: quartz, mica, feldspar
FORMED: deep beneath mountains
FEATURES: wavy surface, with a silvery shimmer

Serpentinite

MINERALS: pyroxene, garnet, hornblende, antigorite
FORMED: deep in Earth's crust
FEATURES: bright red and dark green colors

Green marble

MINERALS: calcite
FORMED: in areas with igneous rocks
FEATURES: light color, with patches of green or blue

Mylonite

MINERALS: various, mainly quartz
FORMED: near **faults**
FEATURES: thin layers of minerals; light-colored quartz **veins**

Slate

MINERALS: quartz, mica, chlorite
FORMED: beneath mountains
FEATURES: splits into thin layers; may have crystals of pyrite ("fool's gold")

Displaying Rocks

After you have collected some rocks, you might want to display them. Here is some advice on starting your rock display.

- Rocks can be heavy! Use a strong shelf or box for your display.

- Clean your rocks before displaying them. Use an old toothbrush and warm water to remove loose soil and dirt.

- Make card labels for each rock. Write the type of rock and where you found it.

- In a notebook or on your computer, keep a record of all the rock samples you have collected.

Record Breakers

Most Common Rock

Basalt covers most of Earth's surface—almost 75 percent! All ocean beds are made of this igneous rock.

Giant's Causeway in Northern Ireland is made up of huge basalt columns that formed naturally.

Largest Rock

The largest freestanding rock is Ayers Rock in Australia. It is made of sandstone. Ayers Rock is 1,140 feet (348 m) high and more than 2.2 miles (3.5 km) long!

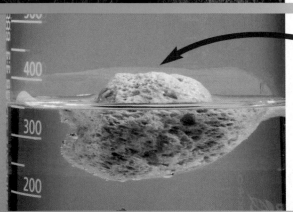

Lightest Rock

The lightest rock is pumice. It is an igneous rock that is formed from bubbly lava. It has many holes in it. Pumice is light enough to float on water!

Oldest Rock

The oldest rock that was formed on Earth is just more than 4 billion years old! It is a metamorphic rock called Acasta gneiss, in the Canadian Shield (see page 13).

Did You Know?

In Hawaii, some beaches have black sand. The sand is made up of volcanic lava.

Scientists have found Mars rocks that landed on Earth. The rocks were broken off the surface of Mars by **asteroids**!

If you drilled deep enough into any of Earth's landmasses, you would find gneiss.

The sedimentary rock limestone is often used for building. The pyramids at Giza in Egypt are made of limestone.

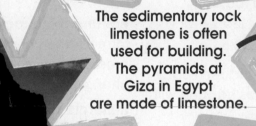

Obsidian is a black rock formed in volcanoes. When it breaks, its edges are very sharp. It has been used for knives and spears.

The metamorphic rock marble is used for statues and monuments. The Leaning Tower of Pisa in Italy is made of marble.

Shiprock Peak in New Mexico towers 1,800 feet (550 m) over the surrounding plain. It was once the central part of a volcano.

Roads are made from very small rock chippings mixed with tar.

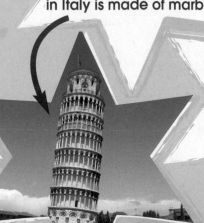

Some of the Moon's surface is made of basalt. This rock, which forms from lava, is also common on Earth.

Glossary

asteroids space rocks that orbit the Sun

crinoid a sea creature that is related to starfish and sea urchins

crystals solid mineral forms with a regular shape

dunes mounds of sand formed by the wind, usually on beaches and in deserts

erosion the carrying away of weathered rocks by moving water, ice, or wind

faults breaks in Earth's crust

flash floods sudden floods that sometimes happen with heavy rainfalls

fossils traces or remains of a living thing from long ago that have been saved in rock

grains tiny pieces of rock that come together to form larger rocks

igneous rocks rocks formed by the hardening of molten material from deep within Earth

lava molten rock on Earth's surface that usually comes out of a volcano

magma molten rock when it is underground

metamorphic rocks rocks formed when heat or pressure, or both, cause changes in rock minerals

minerals naturally formed materials that make up rocks

molten rock rock that is extremely hot and that flows like a liquid

sedimentary rocks rocks formed when small bits of other rocks build up in layers and are squeezed together

veins thin, mineral-filled cracks that run through rocks

volcanoes holes in Earth's crust through which molten rock bursts to the surface

weathering the breakdown of rocks, usually by environmental factors such as ice and plant roots

welded joined by heat or pressure

Index